ALTO SAX

Disney · PIXAR

T0070807

Audio arrangements by Peter Deneff

To access audio visit:
www.halleonard.com/mylibrary

Enter Code
6787-4935-3441-5713

ISBN 978-1-5400-2135-9

HAL•LEONARD®

7777 W. BLUEMOUND RD. P.O. BOX 13819 MILWAUKEE, WI 53213

In Australia Contact:
Hal Leonard Australia Pty. Ltd.
4 Lentara Court
Cheltenham, Victoria, 3192 Australia
Email: ausadmin@halleonard.com.au

Visit Hal Leonard Online at
www.halleonard.com

EVERYONE KNOWS JUANITA

from COCO

ALTO SAX

Music by GERMAINE FRANCO
Lyrics by ADRIAN MOLINA

MUCH NEEDED ADVICE
from COCO

ALTO SAX

Music by MICHAEL GIACCHINO
and GERMAINE FRANCO
Lyrics by ADRIAN MOLINA

LA LLORONA
from COCO

ALTO SAX

Traditional Mexican Folksong
Arranged by GERMAINE FRANCO

PROUD CORAZÓN

from COCO

ALTO SAX

Music by GERMAINE FRANCO
Lyrics by ADRIAN MOLINA

REMEMBER ME
(Ernesto de la Cruz)
from COCO

ALTO SAX

Words and Music by KRISTEN ANDERSON-LOPEZ
and ROBERT LOPEZ

UN POCO LOCO

from COCO

ALTO SAX

Music by GERMAINE FRANCO
Lyrics by ADRIAN MOLINA

THE WORLD ES MI FAMILIA
from COCO

ALTO SAX

Music by GERMAINE FRANCO
Lyrics by ADRIAN MOLINA